A
CHRISTMAS
TREASURY

A
CHRISTMAS
TREASURY

AN ILLUSTRATED CELEBRATION OF CHRISTMAS
IN STORIES, POEMS, AND SONGS

GRAMERCY BOOKS
NEW YORK

This 2003 edition is published by Gramercy Books, an imprint of Random House Value Publishing, a division of Random House, Inc., New York, by arrangement with Michael O'Mara Books Limited.

Gramercy is a registered trademark and the colophon is a trademark of Random House, Inc.

Researched by Jacquie Wines, Vanessa Williams, and Isabel Nohan

The publisher would like to thank Brenda and Gareth Davies and David Drummond for their help in researching illustrative material.

Interior design by Mick Keates • Typeset by Concise Artisans

Picture permissions:
Pages 50, 61, 74, 77, 78, 86, 88 used by permission of Mary Evans Picture Library
Pages 52, 55, 57, 58, 62, 63, 64, 65, 71, 73, 76, 84, 85, 91, 93 used by permission of David Drummond

Text permissions:
Page 60: Extract from *Cider with Rosie* by Laurie Lee, published by Hogarth Press. Used by permission of The Random House Group Limited.

Page 63: Poem used by permission of The Literary Trustees of Walter de la Mare and the Society of Authors as their representative.

Page 71: Extract from Penguin UK edition of *Love for Lydia* by H.E. Bates used by permission of Laurence Pollinger Limited and the Estate of H.E. Bates.

Random House
New York • Toronto • London • Sydney • Auckland
www.randomhouse.com

Printed and bound in Singapore.

A catalog record for this title is available from the Library of Congress.

ISBN 0-517-22154-3

10 9 8 7 6 5 4 3 2 1

Contents

GABRIEL'S MESSAGE

BASQUE CAROL

The angel Gabriel from Heaven came,
His wings as drifted snow, his eyes as flame;
'All hail,' said he, 'thou lowly maiden, Mary,
Most highly favoured lady,' *Gloria!*

'For known a blessed mother thou shalt be,
All generations laud and honour thee,
Thy Son shall be Emmanuel, by seers foretold,
Most highly favoured lady,' *Gloria!*

Then gently Mary meekly bowed her head,
'To me be as it pleaseth God,' she said,
'My soul shall laud and magnify His holy name.'
Most highly favoured lady, *Gloria!*

Of her, Emmanuel, the Christ, was born
In Bethlehem, all on a Christmas morn,
And Christian folk throughout the world will ever say:
Most highly favoured lady, *Gloria!*

WORDS BY REV S. BARING-GOULD

Heap on more wood! – the wind is chill,
But let it whistle as it will,
We'll keep our Christmas merry still.

Sir Walter Scott

A good conscience is a continual Christmas.

Benjamin Franklin

Christmas! 'Tis the season for kindling
the fire of hospitality in the hall, the genial fire
of charity in the heart.

Washington Irving

I will honour Christmas in my heart and try
to keep it all the year.

Charles Dickens

OLD CHRISTMAS

WASHINGTON IRVING

Here were kept up the old games of hoodman blind, shoe the wild mare, hot cockles, steal the white loaf, bob apple, and snapdragon: the Yule-log and Christmas candle were regularly burnt, and the mistletoe, with its white berries, hung up to the imminent peril of the housemaids.

DULCE DOMUM

'I think it must be the field-mice,' replied the Mole, with a touch of pride in his manner...

'Let's have a look at them!' cried the Rat, jumping up and running to the door.

It was a pretty sight, and a seasonable one, that met their eyes when they flung the door open. In the fore-court, lit by the dim rays of a horn lantern, some eight or ten little field-mice stood in a semi-circle, red worsted comforters round their throats, their fore-paws thrust deep into their pockets, their feet jigging for warmth. With bright beady eyes they glanced shyly at each other, sniggering a little, sniffing and applying coat-sleeves a good deal. As the door opened, one of the elder ones that carried the lantern was just saying, 'Now then, one, two, three!' and forthwith their shrill little voices uprose on the air, singing one of the old-time carols that their forefathers composed in fields that were fallow and held by frost, or when snow-bound in chimney corners, and handed down to be sung in the miry streets to lamp-lit windows at Yule-time.

CAROL

Villagers all, this frosty tide,
Let your doors swing open wide,
Though wind may follow, and snow beside,
Yet draw us in by your fire to bide;
Joy shall be yours in the morning!

Here we stand in the cold and the sleet,
Blowing fingers and stamping feet,
Come from far away you to greet —
You by the fire and we in the street —
Bidding you joy in the morning!

For ere one half of the night was gone,
Sudden a star has led us on,
Raining bliss and benison —
Bliss to-morrow and more anon,
Joy for every morning!

Goodman Joseph toiled through the snow —
Saw the star o'er a stable low;
Mary she might not further go —
Welcome thatch, and litter below!
Joy was hers in the morning!

And then they heard the angels tell
'Who were the first to cry Nowell?
Animals all, as it befell,
In the stable where they did dwell!
Joy shall be theirs in the morning!'

KENNETH GRAHAME, *The Wind in the Willows*

9

THE
GLASTONBURY THORN

The legend of the Glastonbury thorn has its origins in Christ's death as well as in the celebration of his birth. The legend goes that soon after the death of Christ, Joseph of Arimathea travelled from the Holy Land to Britain to spread the message of Christianity. Tired out from his journey, he lay down to rest, pushing his staff into the ground beside him. When he awoke, he found that the staff had taken root and had begun to grow and blossom. It is said he left it there and it has flowered every Christmas and every spring. Legend has it that a Puritan who was trying to cut down the tree was prevented from doing so by being blinded by a splinter of the wood as he hacked at it. The original thorn did eventually die but not before many cuttings had been taken. It is one of these very cuttings, they say, which is in the grounds of Glastonbury Abbey today.

No Chamber in the Inn

Anonymous

Yet if his majesty our sovereign lord
Should of his own accord
Friendly himself invite,
And say 'I'll be your guest tomorrow night,'
How should we stir ourselves, call and
    command
All hand to work! 'Let no man idle stand.
Set me fine Spanish tables in the hall,
See they be fitted all;
Let there be room to eat,
And order taken that there want no meat.
See every sconce and candlestick made bright
That without tapers they may give a light.
Look to the presence: are the carpets spread,
The dais o'er the head,
The cushions in the chairs,
And all the candles lighted on the stairs?
Perfume the chambers, and in any case
Let each man give attendance in his place.'
Thus if the king were coming would we do,
And 'twere good reason too;

For 'tis a duteous thing
To show all honour to an earthly king,
And after all our travail and our cost,
So he be pleased, to think no labour cost.
But at the coming of the King of Heaven
All's set at six and seven:
We wallow in our sin,
Christ cannot find a chamber in the inn.
We entertain him always like a stranger,
And as at first still lodge him in the manger.

11

CHRISTMAS-TREE LAND

MRS MOLESWORTH

And there it was – the most beautiful they had yet seen – all radiant with light and glistening with every pretty present child-heart could desire.

'We are only to look at it, you know,' said Maia; 'it has to be packed up and sent us, like the others. But,' she stopped short, 'who is that, Rollo,' she went on, 'standing just by the tree? Can it be Santa Claus himself come to see if it is all right?'

'Santa Claus,' exclaimed a well-known voice, 'Santa Claus, indeed! Is that your new name for me, my Maia?'

Then came a cry of joy – a cry from two little loving hearts – a cry which rang merry echoes through the forest, and at which, though it woke up lots of little birds snugly hidden away in the warmest corners they could find, no one thought of grumbling, except, I think, an old owl, who greatly objected to any disturbance of his nightly promenades and meditations.

'Papa, papa, dear papa!' was the cry. 'Papa, you have come back to us. That was what godmother meant,' they said together. And their father, well pleased, held them in his arms as if he would never let them go.

O CHRISTMAS TREE

O Christmas tree, O Christmas tree!
How are thy leaves so verdant!
O Christmas tree, O Christmas tree,
How are thy leaves so verdant!
Not only in the summertime,
But even in winter is thy prime.
O Christmas tree, O Christmas tree,
How are thy leaves so verdant!
O Christmas tree, O Christmas tree,
Much pleasure doth thou bring me!
O Christmas tree, O Christmas tree,
Much pleasure doth thou bring me!
For every year the Christmas tree,
Brings to us all both joy and glee.
O Christmas tree, O Christmas tree,
Much pleasure doth thou bring me!
O Christmas tree, O Christmas tree,
Thy candles shine out brightly!
O Christmas tree, O Christmas tree,
Thy candles shine out brightly!
Each bough doth hold its tiny light,
That makes each toy to sparkle bright.
O Christmas tree, O Christmas tree,
Thy candles shine out brightly!

THE BIRTH OF CHRIST

as told by SAINT LUKE

And she brought forth her first-born son, and wrapped him in swaddling clothes, and laid him in a manger; because there was no room for them in the inn.

And there were in the same country shepherds abiding in the field, keeping watch over their flock by night.

And, lo, the angel of the Lord came upon them, and the glory of the Lord shone around about them; and they were sore afraid.

And the angel said unto them, Fear not: for, behold, I bring you good tidings of great joy, which shall be to all people.

For unto to you is born this day in the city of David a Saviour, which is Christ the Lord.

And this shall be a sign unto you; ye shall find the babe wrapped in swaddling clothes, lying in a manger.

And suddenly there was with the angel a multitude of the heavenly host praising God, and saying,

Glory to God in the highest, and on earth peace, good will toward men.

LUKE 2: 7-14

JOY TO THE WORLD

Joy to the world! The Lord is come:
Let earth receive her King.
Let ev'ry heart prepare Him room,
And heaven and nature sing,
And heaven and nature sing,
And heaven and heaven and nature sing.

He rules the world with truth and grace,
And makes the nations prove
The glories of His righteousness
And wonders of His love,
And wonders of His love,
And wonders, wonders of His love.

A CHRISTMAS CAROL

CHARLES DICKENS

'A merry Christmas, Uncle! God save you!' cried a cheerful voice. It was the voice of Scrooge's nephew, who came upon him so quickly that this was the first intimation he had of his approach.

'Bah!' said Scrooge. 'Humbug!'

He had so heated himself with rapid walking in the fog and frost, this nephew of Scrooge's, that he was all in a glow; his face was ruddy and handsome; his eyes sparkled, and his breath smoked again.

'Christmas a humbug, Uncle!' said Scrooge's nephew. 'You don't mean that, I am sure?'

'I do,' said Scrooge. 'Merry Christmas! What right have you to be merry? What reason have you to be merry? You're poor enough.'

'Come, then,' returned the nephew gaily. 'What right have you to be dismal? What reason have you to be morose? You're rich enough.'

Scrooge having no better answer ready on the spur of the moment, said, 'Bah!' again; and followed it up with 'Humbug'.

OLD CHRISTMAS

WASHINGTON IRVING

Now Christmas is come,
Let us beat up the drum,
And call all our neighbours together;
And when they appear,
Let us make them such cheer
As will keep out the wind and the weather.

ADVENT WREATHS

The origins of the Advent wreath are found in the folk practices of the pre-Christian Germanic peoples who, during the cold December darkness of Eastern Europe, gathered wreaths of evergreen and lighted fires as signs of hope in a coming spring and renewed light. Christians kept these popular traditions alive, and by the sixteenth century Catholics and Protestants throughout Germany used these symbols to celebrate their Advent hope in Christ, the everlasting Light. From Germany the use of the Advent wreath spread to other parts of the Christian world.

O Come, O Come, Emmanuel

translation by T. A. Lacey

O come, O come, Emmanuel!
Redeem thy captive Israel,
That into exile drear has gone,
Far from the face of God's dear Son.
Rejoice! Rejoice! Emmanuel
Shall come to thee, O Israel.

O come, thou branch of Jesse! Draw
The quarry from the lion's claw:
From the dread caverns of the grave,
From nether hell, thy people save .
Rejoice! . . .

O come, O come, thou Dayspring bright!
Pour on our souls thy healing light;
Dispel the long night's lingering gloom,
And pierce the shadows of the tomb.
Rejoice! . . .

O come, thou Lord of David's Key,
The royal door fling wide and free;
Safeguard for us the heavenward road,
And bar the way to death's abode.
Rejoice! . . .

O come, O come, Adonaï!
Who in thy glorious majesty
From that high mountain, clothed in awe,
Gavest thy folk the elder Law.
Rejoice! . . .

A PRAYER

MARTIN LUTHER

Ah, dearest Jesus, holy Child,
Make thee a bed, soft, undefiled,
Within my heart, that it may be
A quiet chamber kept for Thee.
My heart for very joy doth leap,
My lips no more can silence keep,
I too must sing, with joyful tongue,
That sweetest ancient cradle song,
Glory to God in highest heaven,
Who unto man His Son hath given
While angels sing with pious mirth.
A glad new year to all the earth.

INFANT HOLY

Infant holy, infant lowly
For His bed a cattle stall
Oxen lowing, little knowing
Christ the Babe is Lord of all
Swift are winging, angels singing
Nowells ringing, tidings bringing
Christ the Babe is Lord of all
Flocks were sleeping, shepherds keeping
Vigil till the morning new
Saw the glory, heard the story
Tidings of a gospel true
Thus rejoicing, free from sorrow
Praises voicing, greet the new
Christ the Babe was born for you.

A CHRISTMAS TREE

CHARLES DICKENS

I have been looking on, this evening, at a merry company of children assembled round that pretty German toy, a Christmas Tree. The tree was planted in the middle of a great round table, and towered high above their heads. It was brilliantly lighted by a multitude of little tapers; and everywhere sparkled and glittered with bright objects.

Christmas Tree Legends

It seems to be generally recognized that the people who lived in what is now Germany were the first to develop the tradition of the Christmas tree. Many legends exist about its origins. One is the story of Saint Boniface, an English monk who organized the Christian Church in France and Germany. One day, travelling through Germany, he came upon a group of pagans gathered around a great oak tree about to sacrifice a child to their god. In anger, and to stop the sacrifice and save the child's life, Boniface felled the tree with one mighty blow of his fist. In its place grew a small fir tree. The saint told the pagan worshippers that the tiny fir was the Tree of Life and stood for the eternal life of Christ.

Another legend tells of a poor woodsman who long ago met a lost and hungry child on Christmas Eve. Though very poor himself, the woodsman gave the child food and shelter for the night. The next morning the man awoke to find a beautiful glittering tree outside his door. The hungry child, it was said, was really the Christ Child in disguise. He created the tree to reward the good man for his charity.

Others feel the origin of the Christmas tree may lie in the medieval Paradise Play. Most people in those days could not read and, all over Europe, plays were used to teach the lessons of the Bible. The Paradise Play, which showed the creation of man and the fall of Adam and Eve from the Garden of Eden was performed every year on 24 December. As it was winter, there was a slight problem: an apple tree was needed, but apple trees do not bear fruit – or leaves – in winter so an evergreen was hung about with apples and used instead. Nowadays, the baubles hung on Christmas trees often include shiny red apples.

Martin Luther is credited with first placing candles on the Christmas tree. After his banishment from the Catholic church he spent a great deal of time walking through the forests of evergreen conifers thinking through his beliefs. He was awed by the beauty of millions of stars glimmering through the trees, and was so taken by the sight that he cut a small tree and took it home to his family. To recreate the effect of the stars, he placed candles on all its branches.

THE CHRISTMAS TREE
ACROSS THE WORLD

Early Christmas trees, harking back to pre-Christian times, had, in place of angels, figures of fairies – the good spirits – while horns and bells were placed on it to frighten off evil spirits.

In POLAND, Christmas trees were always decorated with angels, peacocks and other birds as well as many, many stars. In SWEDEN, trees are decorated with brightly painted wooden ornaments and straw figures of animals and children. In DENMARK, tiny Danish flags, along with mobiles of bells, stars, snowflakes and hearts are hung on Christmas trees. JAPANESE Christians prefer tiny fans and paper lanterns. LITHUANIANS cover their trees with straw bird cages, stars, and geometric shapes. The straw sends a wish for good crops in the coming year. CZECHOSLOVAKIAN trees display ornaments made from painted egg shells. In the UKRAINE every Christmas tree has a spider and web for good luck. Legend has it that a poor woman with nothing to put on her children's tree woke on Christmas morning to find the branches covered with spider webs turned to silver by the rising sun.

In BRITAIN, the custom of a decorated Christmas tree appears to have started in the early nineteenth century, when Albert, the Prince Consort to Queen Victoria, brought the tradition from his homeland of Saxe-Coburg, now part of Germany. The example set by royalty became a general fashion.

THE CHRISTMAS STAR

In POLAND, they hold the Festival of the Star. Right after the Christmas Eve meal, the village priest acts as the 'Star Man' and tests the children's knowledge of religion. In ALASKA, boys and girls carry a star-shaped figure from house to house and sing carols in hopes of receiving treats. In HUNGARY a star-shaped pattern is carved in a half of an apple and is supposed to bring good luck.

IN THE BLEAK MID-WINTER

Christina Rossetti

In the bleak mid-winter
Frosty wind made moan,
Earth stood hard as iron,
Water like a stone;
Snow had fallen, snow on snow
Snow on snow,
In the bleak mid-winter,
Long ago.

Our God, heav'n cannot hold Him
Nor earth sustain;
Heav'n and earth shall flee away
When He comes to reign;
In the bleak mid-winter
A stable place sufficed
The Lord God Almighty
Jesus Christ.

Enough for Him, whom Cherubim
Worship night and day,
A breastful of milk,
And a mangerful of hay;
Enough for Him, whom angels
Fall down before,
The ox and ass and camel
Which adore.

What can I give him,
Poor as I am?
If I were a shepherd
I would bring a lamb;
If I were a wise man
I would do my part;
Yet what I can I give Him
Give my heart.

THE GLOW-WORM'S GIFT

At the time of the Nativity, legend tells us, the glow-worm did not possess the light which today is its distinguishing feature. A small, inconspicuous brown beetle, it went about its life unnoticed among the leaves and the grass. And would have remained so if one of them had not happened to be in a field by the stable at the time of Christ's birth. The little insect realized something very wonderful had taken place when she heard the angels singing and saw the shepherds stumbling through the fields in a hurry to see the infant Jesus. From the bigger insects she heard how, from all around, people and animals were flocking to the stable, and how the Wise Men were coming from the East, all bearing gifts to lay before the newborn King. She longed to join in the worship, even though she knew it would be a long and difficult journey across the field for a creature as small as herself. And she had no offering to take Him. But she so wanted to go, and then she remembered she had one prized possession – a hayseed. She could take that. But, she asked herself, what use would it be to the holy Baby, to the King of Heaven? It was all she had, though, and perhaps He would know this, and would not scorn her offering.

So she set off, pushing and dragging the hayseed, struggling through the thick forest of grass and weeds. After many exhausting days, she reached the stable, where she had an arduous climb up into the manger. But, at last, unseen by the crowd of worshippers, she reached the Christ Child and laid her minute gift next to him. No one else saw it, but the Baby did. He gurgled and stretched out His hand, and gently touched the tiny creature that had made such a laborious journey for Him. And as His finger fell softly upon her, her drab little body suddenly glowed with a shining light.

A Christmas Tree

Charles Dickens

Encircled by the social thoughts of Christmas-time, still let the benignant figure of my childhood stand unchanged. In every cheerful image and suggestion the season brings, may the bright star that rested above the poor roof, be the star of all the Christian world!

THE MAGI VISIT THE CHRIST CHILD

Then Herod, when he had privily called the wise men, enquired of them diligently what time the star had appeared.

And he sent them to Bethlehem, and said, Go and search diligently for the young child; and when ye have found him, bring me word again, that I may come and worship him also.

When they had heard the king, they departed; and, lo, the star which they saw in the east, went before them, till it came and stood over where the young child was.

When they saw the star, they rejoiced with exceeding great joy.

And when they were come into the house, they saw the young child with Mary his mother, and fell down, and worshipped him: and when they had opened their treasures, they presented unto him gifts; gold, and frankincense, and myrrh.

And being warned of God in a dream that they should not return to Herod, they departed into their own country another way.

MATTHEW 2: 7-12

A HYMN ON THE NATIVITY OF MY SAVIOUR

I sing the birth was born tonight,
The Author both of life and light;
The angels so did sound it,
And like the ravished shepherds said,
Who saw the light, and were afraid,
Yet searched, and true they found it.

BEN JONSON

O HOLY NIGHT

O holy night!
The stars are brightly shining
It is the night of the dear Saviour's birth!
Long lay the world in sin and error pining,
Till he appear'd and the soul felt its worth.
A thrill of hope the weary world rejoices
For yonder breaks a new and glorious morn!
Fall on your knees
O hear the angel voices
O night divine
O night when Christ was born
O night divine
O night divine.
Led by the light of Faith serenely beaming,
With glowing hearts by His cradle we stand.
So led by light of a star sweetly gleaming,
Here come the wise men from Orient land.
The King of Kings lay thus in lowly manger,
In all our trials born to be our friend.
Truly He taught us to love one another.
His law is love and His gospel is peace.
Chains shall He break, for the slave is our brother
And in His name all oppression shall cease.
Sweet hymns of joy in grateful chorus raise we,
Let all within us praise His holy name.

THE SWORD IN THE STONE

T. H. WHITE

It was Christmas night in the Castle of the Forest Sauvage, and all around the castle the snow lay as it ought to lie. It hung heavily on the battlements, like extremely thick icing on a very good cake, and in a few convenient places it modestly turned itself into the clearest icicles of the greatest possible length. It hung on the boughs of the forest trees in rounded lumps, even better than apple-blossom, and occasionally slid off the roofs of the village when it saw a chance of falling upon some amusing character and giving pleasure to all.

The boys made snowballs with it, but never put

stones in them to hurt each other, and the dogs, when they were taken out to scombre, bit and rolled in it, and looked surprised but delighted when they vanished into deeper drifts. There was skating on the moat, which roared all day with the gliding steel, while hot chestnuts and spiced mead were served on the bank to all and sundry. The owls hooted. The cooks put out all the crumbs they could for the small birds. The villagers brought out their red mufflers. Sir Ector's face shone redder even than these. And reddest of all shone the cottage fires all down the main street of an evening, while the winds howled outside and the old English wolves wandered about slavering in an appropriate manner, or sometimes peeping in at the keyholes with their blood-red eyes.

SUSSEX CAROL

On Christmas night all Christians sing,
To hear the news the angels bring –
News of great joy, news of great mirth,
News of our merciful King's birth.

Then why should men on earth be so sad,
Since our Redeemer made us glad,
When from our sin he set us free,
All for to gain our liberty?

When sin departs before his grace,
Then life and health come in its place:
Angels and men with joy may sing,
All for to see the newborn King.

All out of darkness we have light,
Which made the angels sing this night:
'Glory to God and peace to men,
Now and for evermore. Amen.'

CHRIST'S NATIVITY

HENRY VAUGHAN

Awake, glad heart! Get up and sing,
It is the birthday of thy King,
Awake! Awake!
The sun doth shake
Light from his locks, and all the way
Breathing perfumes, doth spice the day.

MISTLETOE

Mistletoe was thought to be sacred by ancient Europeans. Druid priests employed it in their sacrifices to the gods, while Celtic people believed it to possess miraculous healing powers: in fact, in the Celtic language 'mistletoe' means 'all-heal'. It not only cured diseases, but could also render poisons harmless, make humans and animals prolific, keep one safe from witchcraft, protect the house from ghosts and even make them speak. With all of this, it was thought to bring good luck to anyone privileged to have it.

In a Norse myth, the story goes that mistletoe was the sacred plant of Frigga, goddess of love and the mother of Balder, the god of the summer sun. Balder had a dream of death, which greatly alarmed his mother, for should he die, all life on earth would end. In an attempt to keep this from happening, Frigga went at once to air, fire, water, earth, and every animal and plant, seeking a promise that no harm would come to her son. Balder now could not be hurt by anything on earth or under the earth.

But Balder had one enemy, Loki, the god of evil, and he knew of one plant that Frigga had overlooked in her quest to keep her son safe. It grew neither on the earth nor under the earth, but on apple and oak trees. The lowly mistletoe. So Loki made an arrow tip of the mistletoe, which he gave to the blind god of winter, Hoder, who shot it, striking Balder dead. The sky paled and all things in earth and heaven wept for the sun god. For three days each element tried to bring Balder back to life. From the underworld was brought the message that if everybody wept for Balder he would be allowed to return to earth. And everywhere all living things wept, the mistletoe most of all, its tears becoming pearly white berries, while in her gratitude Frigga kissed everyone who passed beneath the tree on which it grew. The story ends with a decree that who should ever stand under the humble mistletoe, no harm should befall them, only a kiss, a token of love.

Later, the eighteenth-century English credited mistletoe not with miraculous healing powers, but with a certain magical appeal called a kissing ball. At Christmas time a young lady standing under a ball of mistletoe, brightly trimmed with evergreens, ribbons, and ornaments, cannot refuse to be kissed. Such a kiss could mean deep romance or lasting friendship and goodwill. If the girl remained unkissed, she might not expect to marry the following year. Whether we believe it or not, it always makes for fun and frolics at Christmas celebrations.

IVY

Ivy has been a symbol of eternal life in the pagan world and then came to represent new promise and eternal life in the Christian world.

ROSEMARY

Rosemary is yet another Christmas green. Though now it is used mainly to flavour foods, during the Middle Ages it was spread on the floor at Christmas. As people walked on it, the fragrant smell rose up to fill the house. The story goes that Mary laid the garments of the Christ Child over the shrub, which gave it its aroma. It is also said that rosemary is extremely offensive to evil spirits, thus being well suited to the advent of their Conqueror. In addition, the name rosemary associated as it is with the Virgin Mary's name, makes it all the more fitting for the Christmas season.

THE CHRISTMAS ROSE

The Christmas rose, sometimes called the snow or winter rose, is in fact not a rose at all, but a hellebore. It blooms in the depths of winter in the mountains of Central Europe, but may be found in many English gardens. Legend links it with the birth of Christ and a little shepherdess named Madelon.

As Madelon tended her sheep one cold and wintry night, wise men and other shepherds passed by the snow-covered field where she was with their gifts for the Christ Child. The wise men carried the rich gifts of gold, myrrh and frankincense, and the shepherds, fruits, honey and doves. Poor Madelon began to weep for she had nothing at all for the newborn King. An angel, seeing her tears, flew down and before her astonished eyes brushed away the snow revealing a most beautiful white flower tipped with pink – the Christmas rose.

Unto Us is Born a Son

Unto us is born a son!
King of all creation.
Came he to a world forlorn,
The Lord of ev'ry nation.
Cradled in a stall was he,
With sleepy cows and asses;
But the very beasts could see
That he all men surpasses.
Herod then with fear was filled:
'A prince,' he said, 'in Jewry!'

All the little boys he killed
At Bethlem in his fury.
Now may Mary's son, who came
So long ago to love us,
Lead us all with hearts aflame
Unto the joys above us.
Omega and Alpha he!
Let the organ thunder,
While the choir with peals of glee
Doth rend the air asunder.

A CHRISTMAS CAROL

GEORGE WITHER

So now is come our joyful feast,
Let every man be jolly;
Each room with ivy leaves is dressed,
And every post with holly.
Though some churls at our mirth repine,
Round your foreheads garlands twine,
Drown sorrow in a cup of wine,
And let us all be merry.

DECK THE HALL

Deck the hall with boughs of holly, Fa la la la la la la la la!
'Tis the season to be jolly, Fa la la la la la la la la!
Don we now our gay apparel, Fa la la la la la la la la!
Troll the ancient Yuletide carol, Fa la la la la la la la la!

See the blazing yule before us, Fa la la la la la la la la!
Strike the harp and join the chorus, Fa la la la la la la la la!
Follow me in merry measure, Fa la la la la la la la la!
While I tell of Yuletide treasure, Fa la la la la la la la la!

Fast away the old year passes, Fa la la la la la la la la!
Hail the new, ye lads and lasses, Fa la la la la la la la la!
Sing we joyous all together! Fa la la la la la la la la!
Heedless of the wind and weather, Fa la la la la la la la la!

HOLLY

Druids believed that holly, with its shiny leaves and red berries, stayed green to keep the earth beautiful when the sacred oak lost it leaves. They wore sprigs of holly in their hair when they went into the forest to watch their priests cut the sacred mistletoe.

Holly was the sacred plant of Saturn and was used at the Roman Saturnalia festival to honour him. Romans gave one another holly wreaths and carried them about, decorating images of Saturn with it. Centuries later, in December, while other Romans continued their pagan worship,

Christians celebrated the birth of Jesus. To avoid persecution, they decked their homes with Saturnalia holly. As Christian numbers increased and their customs prevailed, holly lost its pagan association and became a symbol of Christmas.

The plant has come to stand for peace and joy, people are said to settle arguments under a holly tree. It is believed to frighten off witches and protect the home from thunder and lightning. In GERMANY, a piece that has been used in church decorations is regarded as a charm

against lightning. In western ENGLAND it is said that sprigs of holly around a young girl's bed on Christmas Eve are supposed to keep away mischievous goblins. And some British farmers put sprigs of holly on their beehives. On the first Christmas, they believed, the bees hummed in honour of the Christ Child. The English also mention the 'he holly and the she holly' as being the determining factor in who will rule the household in the following year, the 'she holly' having smooth leaves and the 'he holly' having prickly ones.

Other beliefs included putting a sprig of holly on the bedpost to bring sweet dreams and making a tonic from holly to cure a cough. Enough reasons for decking the hall with boughs of holly.

ON THE MORNING OF CHRIST'S NATIVITY

JOHN MILTON

This is the month, and this the happy morn
Wherein the Son of Heav'n's eternal King,
Of wedded Maid, and Virgin Mother born,
Our great redemption from above did bring;
For so the holy sages once did sing,
That he our deadly forfeit should release,
And with his Father work us a perpetual peace.

THE POINSETTIA

The legend of the poinsettia comes from Mexico. It tells of a girl named Maria and her little brother Pablo. They were very poor but always looked forward to the Christmas festival. Each year a large manger scene was set up in the village church, and the days before Christmas were filled with parades and parties. The two children loved Christmas but were always saddened because they had no money to buy presents. They especially wished that they could give something to the church for the Baby Jesus. But they had nothing.

One Christmas Eve, Maria and Pablo set out for church to attend the service. On their way they picked some weeds growing along the roadside and decided to take them as their gift to the Baby Jesus in the manger scene. Of course, other children teased them when they arrived with their gift, but they said nothing, for they knew they had given what they could. Maria and Pablo began placing the green plants around the manger and, miraculously, the green top leaves turned into bright red petals, and soon the manger was surrounded by beautiful star-like flowers and so we see them today.

FATHER CHRISTMAS

Santa Claus, legendary bringer of gifts at Christmas, is generally depicted as a fat, jolly man with a white beard, dressed in a red suit trimmed with white, and driving a sleigh full of toys, drawn through the air by eight reindeer. Santa (also called Saint Nicholas and Saint Nick) is said to visit on Christmas Eve, entering houses through the chimney to leave presents under the Christmas tree and in the stockings of all good children. Although this familiar image of Santa Claus is a North American invention of the nineteenth century, it has ancient European roots and continues to influence the celebration of Christmas throughout the world.

The historical Saint Nicholas – Sankt Nikolaus in Germany and Sanct Herr Nicholaas or

Sinter Klaas in Holland – was venerated in early Christian legend for saving storm-tossed sailors, defending young children, and giving generous gifts to the poor. Although many of the stories about Saint Nicholas are of doubtful authenticity (for example, he is said to have delivered a bag of gold to a poor family by tossing it through a window), his legend spread throughout Europe, emphasizing his role as a traditional bringer of gifts. The Christian figure of Saint Nicholas replaced or incorporated various pagan gift-giving figures such as the Roman Befana and the Germanic Berchta and Knecht Ruprecht. In some countries Nicholas was said to ride through the sky on a horse. He was depicted wearing a bishop's robes and was said to be accompanied at times by Black Peter, an elf whose job was to whip any naughty children.

IT WAS ON CHRISTMAS DAY

It was on Christmas Day,
And all in the morning,
Our Saviour was born,
And our heavenly king:
And was not this a joyful thing?
And sweet Jesus they called him by name.

ANON

THE LEGEND OF THE BEASTS IN THE STABLE

It is said that in the stable where Mary bore Jesus, alongside the donkey that had carried her to Bethlehem, there were also some oxen sheltering from the winter cold. That evening the animals were all given some hay, but they didn't eat it, knowing that it would be needed to make a bed for the soon-to-be-born baby.

Once the child arrived, the beasts gathered around and breathed on him gently to keep him warm, and when the shepherds came to worship the babe, the animals too knelt down before the manger. Later, the donkey noticed some mice and rats in the stable and he was concerned for the baby, and started to bray to keep them away. But this woke the baby, so the oxen began to low softly to lull him back to sleep.

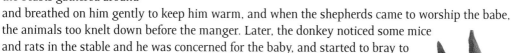

It is said that to repay the animals for their loving kindness, they were granted the power of human speech every year at the midnight that comes between Christmas Eve and Christmas Day. Some believe that this is still so, and that every Christmas Eve, at midnight, the animals in the fields kneel down to worship the Christ child.

BETHLEHEM OF JUDEA

A little child,
A shining star.
A stable rude,
The door ajar.

Yet in that place,
So crude, forlorn,
The Hope of all
The world was born.

ANON

I Saw Three Ships
Come Sailing In

I saw three ships come sailing in
On Christmas Day, on Christmas Day.
I saw three ships come sailing in
On Christmas Day in the morning.

And what was in those ships all three
On Christmas Day, on Christmas Day?
And what was in those ships all three
On Christmas Day in the morning?

Our Saviour Christ and His lady
On Christmas Day, on Christmas Day.
Our Saviour Christ and His lady,
On Christmas Day in the morning.

Pray whither sailed those ships all three
On Christmas Day, on Christmas Day?
Pray whither sailed those ships all three
On Christmas Day in the morning?

O, they sailed in to Bethlehem
On Christmas Day, on Christmas Day.
O they sailed in to Bethlehem
On Christmas Day in the morning.

And all the bells on earth shall ring
On Christmas Day, on Christmas Day.
And all the bells on earth shall ring
On Christmas Day in the morning.

And all the angels in Heav'n shall sing
On Christmas Day, on Christmas Day.
And all the angels in Heav'n shall sing
On Christmas Day in the morning.

And all the souls on earth shall sing
On Christmas Day, on Christmas Day;
And all the souls on earth shall sing
On Christmas Day in the morning.

Then let us all rejoice again
On Christmas Day, on Christmas Day.
Then let us all rejoice again
On Christmas Day in the morning.

WORDS: ENGLISH TRADITIONAL

GOOD KING WENCESLAUS

There actually was a King Wenceslaus. He was born in about AD 903 into the Premys family, who were the most able of the Bohemian nobles, and who ruled over various tribes. Bohemia, which was then a duchy rather than a kingdom, had forged links with the German Holy Roman Emperor and the Duke supported and encouraged the spread of Christianity.

However, Wenceslaus's mother, Dragomir, was a pagan, and she was violently against her husband's beliefs. She eventually overthrew him and had many Christian missionaries killed. But she was, in turn, overthown, and the Christian Wenceslaus, as the eldest son, was installed as Duke. Dragomir did not accept this course of events and encouraged her younger son, Boleslav, to wage war on Wenceslaus. This he did, but legend has it that Wenceslaus was protected by an angelic bodyguard during battle.

Wenceslaus won and he recalled the German missionaries and promoted Christian beliefs throughout Bohemia. He became famous for his generosity, charitable deeds and selfless behaviour.

As tradition has it, on the feast of Stephen – which falls on 26th December and commemorates St Stephen, the first Christian martyr – Wenceslaus stood at his castle window looking out at the snowy landscape. Darkness had fallen, but the moon was bright and in its light Wenceslaus could discern the figure of an old man, bent and in rags, who was struggling to pick up firewood.

Wenceslaus was moved with pity for the man and called to his old servant to come to him. He asked the servant if he knew the poor man and where he lived. The servant informed him that he lived against the forest fence near the fountain of St Agnes. Wenceslaus then asked the servant to fetch meat and wine, while he himself shouldered some large logs of wood, and the two of them set off to the poor man's home. The wind was so chill and the snow was so deep that after a time the old servant called out that he could go no farther. But Wenceslaus turned and smiled encouragement on him and told him to walk close behind him so that he would be sheltered from the winter wind and could walk in his footsteps. To the old servant's amazement, he found that when he did as Wenceslaus bade him, the deep snow ceased to hamper him, and despite the shrill whistling of the wind he could continue onwards.

In reward for Wenceslaus's efforts, Emperor Otto I upgraded Bohemia to a kingdom and

presented Wenceslaus with a crown, which can still be seen today. On 28 September 929, as King Wenceslaus was praying, he was ambushed by Boleslav, who murdered him at the church door. Wenceslaus was hailed as a martyr and was canonized and installed as the patron saint of Bohemia. Boleslav was crowned king and ruled until 967. However, he was overcome with remorse at having killed his brother, and converted to Christianity. Therefore, Bohemia remained Christian.

THE STORY OF SILENT NIGHT

In Salzburg, Austria, a weaver called Anna fell in love with a soldier and she conceived a child who was born on 11 December 1792. The soldier wanted nothing to do with his son and he abandoned Anna, leaving her to bring up the boy on her own. She named him Joseph Mohr.

Not only was Joseph an intelligent child, he had a lovely voice. The local priest arranged for him to attend the famous abbey school of Kremsmünster, and later, when he was sixteen, he decided to go into the priesthood. At the age of twenty-two he was assigned to the church of St Nicholas in Oberndorf, just outside Salzburg.

There Joseph became friends with a local music teacher, Franz Gruber, for they both shared a love of music and both played the guitar.

On 23 December 1818, Joseph went to visit a mother and her newborn child. On his way back, he stopped by the river and reflected on the very first Christmas. He wrote a poem to capture his thoughts and called it 'Silent Night'.

On arriving back at the church, he found the parish in a state of alarm. Some mice had nibbled away at the church organ and the villagers were fearful that there would be no music for Midnight Mass the following evening.

Joseph had an idea. He rushed to his friend Franz Gruber and asked if he could compose a melody for the poem he had written, to be played on the guitar. Franz worked on the song and completed it in time for the mass. So it was that Christmas, that the world first heard the well-loved carol that is now sung in many languages across the globe.

SILENT NIGHT

JOSEPH MOHR

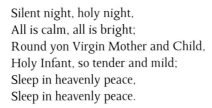

Silent night, holy night,
All is calm, all is bright;
Round yon Virgin Mother and Child,
Holy Infant, so tender and mild;
Sleep in heavenly peace,
Sleep in heavenly peace.

Silent night, holy night,
Shepherds quake at the sight;
Glories stream from heaven afar,
Heavenly hosts sing alleluia;
Christ the Saviour is born,
Christ the Saviour is born.

CAROL SINGING

LAURIE LEE, from *Cider with Rosie*

We grouped ourselves round the farmhouse porch. The sky cleared, and broad streams of stars ran down over the valley and away to Wales. On Slad's white slopes, seen through the black sticks of its woods, some red lamps still burned in the windows.

Everything was quiet; everywhere there was the faint crackling silence of the winter night. We started singing, and we were all moved by the words and the sudden trueness of our voices. Pure, very clear, and breathless we sang:

> *As Joseph was a walking*   *He neither shall be bornèd*
> *He heard an angel sing;*   *In housen nor in hall,*
> *'This night shall be the birth-time*   *Nor in a place of paradise*
> *Of Christ the Heavenly King.*   *But in an ox's stall . . . .'*

And two thousand Christmases became real to us then; the houses, the halls, the places of paradise had all been visited; the stars were bright to guide the Kings through the snow; and across the farmyard we could hear the beasts in their stalls. We were given roast apples and hot mince-pies, in our nostrils were spices like myrrh, and in our wooden box, as we headed back for the village, there were golden gifts for all.

Deck the Halls with Boughs of Holly

We often use foliage to decorate our homes at Christmas. Green foliage symbolizes the continuance of life through the dark winter months, and in a Christian context the eternal life offered to us by Christ. The tradition of placing a wreath of greenery on the door of the house probably dates back to Roman times, when wreaths were hung as a sign of spring's victory over winter.

Holly also has a symbolic meaning. The prickly leaves of the holly bush represent the crown of thorns worn by Jesus at his crucifixion and the red berries symbolize the drops of blood that he shed. Mistletoe was considered by Celtic druids to be a sacred plant and sprigs of it were used as charms. Its dark green leaves and white berries are often found hanging from the ceiling at Christmas, but be careful — anyone who wants to kiss you may do so if you are standing under the mistletoe.

MISTLETOE

WALTER DE LA MARE

Sitting under the mistletoe
(Pale green, fairy mistletoe),
One last candle burning low,
All the sleepy dancers gone,
Just one candle burning on,
Shadows lurking everywhere:
Some one came, and kissed me there.

Tired I was; my head would go
Nodding under the mistletoe
(Pale green, fairy mistletoe),
No footsteps came, no voice, but only,
Just as I sat there, sleepy, lonely,
Stooped in the still and shadowy air
Lips unseen – and kissed me there.

THE SHEPHERD
WHO STAYED BEHIND

On the night when Jesus was born, there were shepherds in the fields around Bethlehem tending their flocks. Suddenly a mighty throng of angels appeared to them and bade them go visit the Christ child.

The shepherds hurried away, but one shepherd, Shemuel, stayed behind. He longed to join the others as they rushed down the hillside and into the town, but earlier in the evening he had found a sick man lost in the hills. Shemuel had cared for him all night. The man was certainly close to death and it would not be fair to leave him.

When the other shepherds came back from the town telling of the babe in the stable who would be Lord of All, Shemuel was filled with great sadness that he had not been there.

Soon afterwards he became ill with the stranger's fever, and realized that he too was going to die. He was terrified and bitter at his fate. However, as Shemuel lay on the ground a most wondrous sight appeared above him. There in the sky was a vision of God the Father, God the Son and God the Holy Ghost, seated on high.

As he gazed, all of Shemuel's fear and disquiet left him. Although he had been unable to see the Christ child, he was the first among men to be shown the Holy Trinity. Shemuel closed his eyes and his spirit left him and was guided up to Heaven by the angels.

Softly the Night

Softly the night is sleeping on Bethlehem's peaceful hill,
Silent the shepherds watching their gentle flocks are still.
But hark the wondrous music falls from the opening sky,
Valley and cliff re-echo glory to God on high.
Glory to God it rings again,
Peace on the earth, goodwill to men.

Come with the gladsome shepherds quick hastening from the fold,
Come with the wise men bringing incense and myrrh and gold,
Come to him poor and lowly all round the cradle throng,
Come with our hearts of sunshine and sing the angels' song.
Glory to God tell out again,
Peace on the earth, goodwill to men.

Wave you the wreath unfading, the fir tree and the pine,
Green from the snows of winter to deck the holy shrine;
Bring you the happy children for this is Christmas morn,
Jesus the sinless infant, Jesus the Lord is born.
Glory to God, to God again,
Peace on the earth, goodwill to men.

ANON

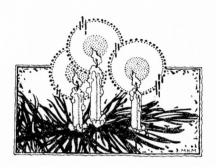

XMAS DAY

G. K. CHESTERTON

Good news: but if you ask me what it is, I know not;
It is a track of feet in the snow,
It is a lantern showing a path,
It is a door set open.

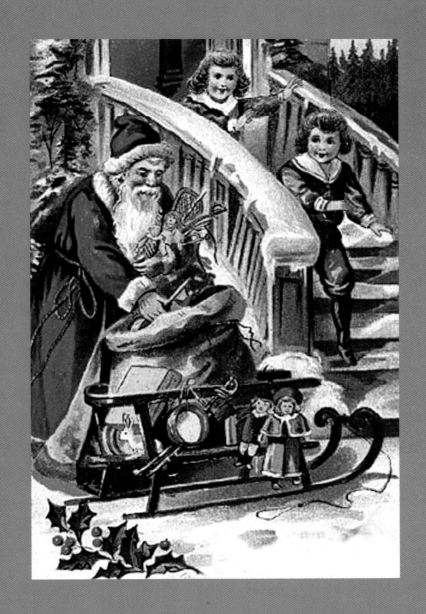

WINTER FESTIVITIES

The middle of winter has long been a time of celebration around the world. Centuries before the birth of Christ, Europeans celebrated light and birth in the darkest days of winter. Many people rejoiced during the winter solstice when the worst of the winter was behind them and they could look forward to longer days and extended hours of sunlight.

The end of December was a perfect time for celebration in most areas of Europe. At that time of year, most cattle were slaughtered so that they did not have to be fed during winter. For many, it was the only time of the year when they had a supply of fresh meat. In addition, most wine and beer was finally fermented and ready for drinking.

In Rome, where winters were not as harsh as those in the far north, Saturnalia, a holiday in honour of Saturn, the god of agriculture, was celebrated. Beginning in the week leading up to the winter solstice and continuing for a full month, Saturnalia was a hedonistic time, when food and drink were plentiful.

Around the time of the winter solstice, Romans also observed Juvenalia, a feast honouring the children of Rome. In addition, members of the upper classes often celebrated the birthday of Mithra, the god of the unconquerable sun, on December 25. It was believed that Mithra, an infant god, was born of a rock. For some Romans, Mithra's birthday was the most sacred day of the year.

WINTER IN-DOORS AND OUT

Out of doors warm hoods and mittens
Cheeks with romping all a-glow
Merry slides and splendid skating
Harmless tumbles in the snow
In the house a cosy nook
And a tempting story book.

Out of doors a snow-man funny
On a sled a journey gay
In the house a smoking dinner
Dolls to dress and games to play
Races in the frosty air
In the house an easy-chair.

Out of doors the cold wind blowing
Snow-drifts piling in the street
In the house the rosy firelight
Rest for weary hands and feet
Darkness out of doors and din
Home and mother safe within.

Anon

WINTER

WILLIAM SHAKESPEARE

When icicles hang by the wall
    And Dick the shepherd blows his nail,
And Tom bears logs into the hall,
    And milk comes frozen home in pail;
When blood is nipt, and ways be foul,
Then nightly sings the staring owl
             Tu-whit!
Tu-who!   A merry note!
While greasy Joan doth keel the pot.

When all about the wind doth blow,
    And coughing drowns the parson's saw,
And birds sit brooding in the snow,
    And Marian's nose looks red and raw;
When roasted crabs hiss in the bowl —
Then nightly sings the staring owl
             Tu-whit!
Tu-who! A merry note!
While greasy Joan doth keel the pot.

SKATING AT CHRISTMAS

H. E. BATES, from *Love for Lydia*

'There'll be skating,' she said. 'That would be wonderful – skating for Christmas. Everybody loves the idea of skating for Christmas. Everybody waits for it and it hardly ever comes.'

We came to a small hill where the road made a passage between spinneys of oak and hazel above the valley of a brook. The delicate branches of hazel, fingered already with pale stiff catkins, were snowless under the high protective screen of oaks. Where the sun caught them the catkins were pale greenish-yellow, almost spring-like, and I could see the primrose leaves piercing a crust of snowy oak-leaf under thin blue shadows. The hill was not very steep but Blackie put the car into lower gear, driving with a new excess of caution, so that we crept down into the valley at less than walking pace, the ghostly, glittering chariot making hardly a sound in the closed avenue of hazels.

Then we were clear of the woods and suddenly, delicate and transfigured and untouched, the river valley of snow-meadows, with small lakes of frozen flood water lying darker about it, was there below us. It appeared so suddenly and was so beautiful, full in sun, the snow deep blue below the paler blue of sky and between the tawny-purple lips of frosty horizons, that she sat bolt upright in her seat and let go my hands.

'Oh! stop – let's stop here! That's so lovely —'

A Christmas Husbandly Fare

Thomas Tusser, 1573

Good husband and huswife, now chiefly be glad.
Things handsome to have, as they ought to be had.
They both do provide, against Christmas do come,
To welcome their neighbours, good chere to have some.

Good bread and good drinks, a good fier in the hall,
Brawne, pudding, and souse, and good mutard withal.
Biefe, mutton, and Porke, and good Pies of the best,
Pig, veale, goose and capon, and turkey wel drest,
Chese, apples and nuttes, and good Caroles to heare,
As then, in the country is counted good cheare.
What cost to good husbande, is any of this?
Good household provision onely it is:
Of other the like, I do leave out a meny,
That costeth a husband never a peny.

IT IS NOW CHRISTMAS...

NICHOLAS BRETON, 1626

It is now Christmas, and not a cup of drink must
pass without a carol: the beasts, fish and fowl come
to a general execution, and the corn is ground to dust
for the bakehouse and the pastry – Now good cheer
and welcome, and God be with you.

Snap-Dragon — a Victorian Christmas game

… a kind of play, in which brandy is set on fire, and raisins thrown into it, which those who are unused to the sport are afraid to take out, but which may be safely snatched by a quick motion and put blazing into the mouth, which being closed, the fire is at once extinguished.

British Popular Customs (1876)

It should be said that the Victorians were much more cavalier about safety than their 21st century counterparts.

CHRISTMAS EVE

WASHINGTON IRVING, from *Old Christmas and Bracebridge Hall*

As we approached the house, we heard the sound of music, and now and then a burst of laughter from one end of the building. This, Bracebridge said, must proceed from the servant's hall, where a great deal of revelry was permitted, and even encouraged, by the Squire throughout the twelve days of Christmas, provided everything was done conformably with ancient usage …

Supper was announced shortly after our arrival. It was served up in a spacious oaken chamber, the panels of which shone with wax, and around which were several family portraits decorated with holly and ivy. Beside the accustomed lights, two great wax tapers, called Christmas candles, wreathed with greens, were placed on a highly-polished buffet among the family plate. The table was abundantly spread with substantial fare; but the Squire made his supper of frumentt, a dish made of wheat cakes boiled in milk with rice spices, being a standing dish in old times for Christmas Eve. I was happy to find my old friend, the minced-pie, in the retinue of the feast; and finding him to be perfectly orthodox, and that I need not be ashamed of predilection, I greeted him with all the warmth wherewith we usually greet an old and very genteel acquaintance.

GLORIOUS PLUM PUDDING

In a household where there are five or six children, the eldest is not above ten or eleven, the making of the pudding is indeed an event. It is thought of days, if not weeks, before. To be allowed to share in the noble work, is a prize for young ambition … Lo! The lid is raised, curiosity stands on tip-toe, eyes sparkle with anticipation, little hands are clapped in extasy, almost too great to find expression in words. 'The hour arrives – the moment wished and feared;' – wished, oh! how intensely; feared, not in the event, but lest envious fate should not allow it to be an event, and mar the glorious concoction in its very birth.

And then when it is dished, when all fears of this kind are over, when the roast beef has been removed, when the pudding, in all the glory of its own splendour, shines upon the table, how eager is the anticipation of the near delight! How beautifully it steams! How delicious it smells! How round it is! A kiss is round, the horizon is round, the earth is round, the moon is round, the sun and stars and all the host of heaven are round. So is plum pudding.

THE ILLUSTRATED LONDON NEWS, December 1848

THE STORY OF THE CHRISTMAS CRACKER

We must thank Tom Smith for the Christmas cracker. Tom was a London confectioner who was always looking for novel ideas. He travelled abroad in search of inspiration and brought back the bonbon to England after a trip to France. His bonbons contained a motto beneath their wrapping – probably a Victorian love poem – and the sweets sold very well, particularly at Christmas. In 1847, Tom was sitting by his fire, musing on ways to increase trade, when the sparks from the crackling logs gave him an idea. He would invent a bonbon that went off with a bang when opened, and inside would be not only a sweet but also a motto and a toy. He named these *cosaques*, but today we still talk of bonbons in connection with Christmas crackers.

Tom Smith enjoyed huge success with his crackers and soon had a royal warrant. He produced crackers not only at Christmas but also for every special occasion, including the Paris Exhibition in 1906 and the Prince of Wales's World Tour in 1926.

LOVE CAME DOWN
AT CHRISTMAS

CHRISTINA ROSSETTI

Love came down at Christmas,
    Love all lovely, love divine,
Love was born at Christmas,
    Star and angels gave the sign.

Worship we the Godhead,
    Love incarnate, love divine;
Worship we our Jesus:
    But wherewith for sacred sign?

Love shall be our token,
    Love be yours and love be mine,
Love to God and all men,
    Love for plea and gift and sign.

TRUCE IN THE TRENCHES, 1914

W. R. M. PERCY, LONDON RIFLE BRIGADE

We had a rather interesting time in the trenches on Christmas Eve and Christmas Day. We were in some places less than a hundred yards from the Germans, and we talked to them. It was agreed in our part of the firing line that there should be no firing and no thought of war on these days, so they sang and played to us several of their own tunes and some of ours, such as 'Home Sweet Home' and 'Tipperary' etc., while we did the same for them.

The regiment on our left all got out of their trenches and every time a flare went up they simply stood there, cheered and waved their hats, and not a shot was fired on them. The singing and playing continued all night, and the next day (Christmas) our fellows paid a visit to the German

trenches and they did likewise. Cigarettes, cigars, addresses etc. were exchanged, and everyone, friend or foe, were real good pals. One of the German officers took a photo of English and German soldiers arm in arm, with exchanged caps and helmets.

On Christmas Eve the Germans burnt coloured lights and candles along the top of their trenches, and on Christmas Day a football match was played between them and us in front of the trench. They even allowed us to bury all our dead lying in front, and some of them, with hats in hand, brought in one of our dead officers from behind their trench so that we could bury him decently. They were really magnificent in the whole thing, and jolly good sorts. I have now a very different opinion of the German. Both sides have now started firing and are deadly enemies again. Strange it all seems, doesn't it?

SOLDIERS' SONG

It was Christmas Day in the cookhouse,
The happiest day of the year,
Men's hearts were full of gladness,
An' their bellies full of beer ...

THE SNOW LIES WHITE

The snow lies white on roof and tree,
Frost fairies creep about,
The world's as still as it can be,
And Santa Claus is out.

He's making haste his gifts to leave,
While the stars show his way,
There'll soon be no more Christmas Eve,
Tomorrow's Christmas Day!

ANON

ST NICHOLAS'S SCARY HELPER

Most people have heard of St Nicholas as Santa Claus or Father Christmas, but few have heard about his scary helper. In the Netherlands he is called Black Peter, in Germany he is Knecht Ruprecht, in France he is known as Pere Fouettard and in Luxembourg they call him Hoesecker.

While St Nicholas comes to give all the good children presents, his helper puts switches in the stockings of the naughty girls and boys for their parents to spank them with. Some say that he even carries away those who have been really naughty in his bag.

EPIPHANY

The word Epiphany comes from the Greek word *epiphaneia*, which means an appearance or a manifestation. In the Greek and Russian orthodox churches, Christmas is celebrated on January 6, which is also referred to as Epiphany or Three Kings Day. This is the day it is believed that the three wise men found Jesus in the stable in Bethlehem.

THE THREE KINGS

The Three Kings are also known as the Wise Men or the Magi. Traditionally they were Caspar, King of Tarsus, the Land of Myrrh; Melchior, King of Arabia, the Land of Gold; and Balthasar, King of Saba, the Land of Frankincense.

The gifts of Gold, Frankincense and Myrrh are all symbolic. Gold symbolizes kingship, and also the gift of charity and spiritual riches embodied in Christ. Frankincense depicts godliness and the gift of faith. Myrrh foretells the painful death of Jesus and the gift of truth and meekness.

Although the Wise Men returned home after visiting Jesus some say they were baptized by St. Thomas and later became Christian martyrs, and that their bodies were buried within the walls of Jerusalem.

Twelfth Night and the Lord of Misrule

Twelfth Night marks Epiphany in the Church's calendar. Through the ages, Twelfth Night has been a time when the existing social order is turned upside-down. This can be found both in the Roman festival of Saturnalia and the Babylonian festival of Sacaea, where servants became masters and the masters had to obey their slaves.

In the fifth century, the churches of France and England carried on this tradition, appointing Bishops and Archbishops of Fools to revel and cause mischief. This continued in England until the Middle Ages, where a beggar or student would be crowned the 'Lord of Misrule' and the poor would go to the homes of the rich and demand the very best food and drink. Failure to comply with this request would probably result in the household being terrorized with mischief.

In the Netherlands, a version of this tradition continues to this day. On 6 January, which is known as *Driekoningendag* or Three Kings Day, an Epiphany cake is baked and whoever finds the bean inside it is king for the day and wears a gold paper crown.

THE YULE LOG

In Scandinavia, because it is so far north, the sun disappears from the sky in the middle of winter. Before people understood why it was dark in winter, they were frightened that one year the sun might go away and never come back, so after thirty-five days of darkness scouts were sent on to the mountains to look out for the return of the sun. When the sun had been sighted, the scouts would return to their villages with the good news and Yuletide would begin. The sons and fathers of families would go out and find a large log, or Yule log, which they would then set on fire. Yuletide celebrations would continue until the log had finished burning – sometimes this could go on for twelve days! The Norse believed that every spark that the fire made represented the birth of a new pig or calf during the next year. As the fire began to die down, a piece of the Yule Log would be taken out and saved until the next year, when it would be used to light the next Yule Log.

CHRISTMAS IN A VILLAGE

JOHN CLARE

Each house is swept the day before,
And windows stuck with evergreens;
The snow is bosomed from the door,
And comfort crowns the cottage scenes.
Gilt holly with its thorny pricks
And yew and box with berries small,
These deck the unused candlesticks,
And pictures hanging by the wall.

Neighbours resume their annual cheer,
Wishing with smiles and spirits high
Glad Christmas and a happy year
To every morning passer-by.
Milkmaids their Christmas journeys go
Accompanied with favoured swain,
And children pace the crumping snow
To taste their granny's cake again.

Hung with the ivy's veining bough,
The ash trees round the cottage farm
Are often stripped of branches now
The cottar's Christmas hearth to warm.
He swings and twists his hazel band,
And lops them off with sharpened hook,
And oft brings ivy in his hand
To decorate the chimney nook . . .

The shepherd now no more afraid,
Since custom does the chance bestow,
Starts up to kiss the giggling maid
Beneath the branch of mistletoe
That 'neath each cottage beam is seen
With pearl-like berries shining gay,
The shadow still of what has been
Which fashion yearly fades away.

And singers too, a merry throng,
At early morn with simple skill
Yet imitate the angel's song
And chant their Christmas ditty still;
And 'mid the storm that dies and swells
By fits – in hummings softly steals
The music of the village bells
Ringing round their merry peals.

And when it's past, a merry crew
Bedecked in masks and ribbons gay,
The morris dance their sports renew
And act their winter evening play.
The clown-turned-king for penny praise
Storms with the actor's strut and swell,
And Harlequin a laugh to raise
Wears his hunchback and tinkling bell.

And oft for pence and spicy ale
With winter nosegays pinned before,
The wassail singer tells her tale
And drawls her Christmas carols o'er,
While prentice boy with ruddy face
And frost-bepowdered dancing locks
From door to door with happy pace
Runs round to claim his Christmas box.

ROBIN REDBREAST'S SONG

There was once a robin with a beautiful voice who wanted to sing for the King on Christmas morning. It was a long way to the castle, but the robin was determined to get there.

He flew and he flew until he came to rest in a tree. Just then a cat came to sharpen its claws on the trunk. 'Good morning Robin Redbreast,' said the cat. 'Where are you going on this cold day?' 'I'm going to the King,' answered the robin, 'to sing him a Christmas song.' 'Oh, but wait before you go,' said the cat. 'Fly down and I'll show you the beautiful collar my owners gave me today.' The robin was tempted, but he saw the cruel gleam in the cat's eye. 'Thank you, good Cat,' he said, 'but I must fly straight on to the King. Merry Christmas to you.'

He flew on and on and finally rested on a fence. There sat a hawk. 'Good morning, Robin Redbreast,' cried the hawk. 'Where are you going on this cold day?' 'I'm going to the King,' answered the robin, 'to sing him a Christmas song.' 'Oh, but wait before you go,' said the hawk. 'Pray spare a moment to see my magic tail feather.' The robin was tempted, but he noticed the way that the hawk was flexing his talons. 'Thank you, good Hawk,' he said, 'but I must fly straight on to the King. Merry Christmas to you.'

So he spread his wings and flew away. He flew, and he flew, and he flew, till he came to a hillside and rested on a mound. A fox looked out from his hole. 'Good morning, Robin Redbreast,' said the fox. 'Where are you going on this cold day?' 'I'm going to the King,' answered the robin, 'to sing him a Christmas song.' 'Wait a while and catch your breath,' said the fox. 'I will come closer and warm you with my winter coat.' The robin was cold and tired, but he saw how the fox was licking his lips. 'Thank you, good Fox,' he said, 'but I must go straight on to the King. Merry Christmas to you.'

So the robin flew away once more, and never rested till he came to a small boy, who sat on a log eating a big piece of bread and butter. The robin was very hungry by now and he hoped that the boy might throw him a crumb. 'Good morning, Robin Redbreast,' said the boy. 'Where are you going on this cold morning?' 'I'm going to sing a Christmas song to the King,' said the robin. 'Come a bit nearer,' said the boy. 'I'll give you some crumbs from my bread.' The robin was very grateful, but suddenly he spotted the stones in the boy's hand.

'Thank you, good Sir,' he said, 'but I must fly straight on to the King. Merry Christmas to you.'

So, no matter who begged him to stop and wait, the robin flew straight on to the King. And finally he alighted on the window-sill of the palace. There he sat and sang the sweetest Christmas song he knew. He wanted the whole world to be as joyful about Christmas as he, and he sang, and he sang, and he sang.

The King and Queen were so pleased with his joyful song that they asked all the courtiers what they could give the robin in return. It was decided that they should find the robin a mate. Thus they brought to him Jenny Wren, who lived in the kitchen courtyard, and the two birds sang all that Christmas and many Christmases thereafter.

GERMAN CAROL

The Christmas tree with lights is gleaming,
And stands in bright and festive glow.
As if to say – Mark well my meaning.
Hope's image green and bright I show.

A Christmas Welcome

Charlotte Brontë, from *Jane Eyre*

'My first aim will be to clean down ... Moor House from chamber to cellar; my next to rub it up with beeswax, oil, and an indefinite number of cloths, till it glitters again; my third, to arrange every chair, table, bed, carpet, with mathematical precision; afterwards I shall go near to ruin you in coals

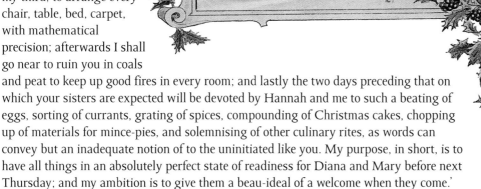

and peat to keep up good fires in every room; and lastly the two days preceding that on which your sisters are expected will be devoted by Hannah and me to such a beating of eggs, sorting of currants, grating of spices, compounding of Christmas cakes, chopping up of materials for mince-pies, and solemnising of other culinary rites, as words can convey but an inadequate notion of to the uninitiated like you. My purpose, in short, is to have all things in an absolutely perfect state of readiness for Diana and Mary before next Thursday; and my ambition is to give them a beau-ideal of a welcome when they come.'

Jane Eyre to St. John Rivers

MOONLESS DARKNESS STANDS BETWEEN

GERARD MANLEY HOPKINS

Moonless darkness stands between.
Past, O Past, no more be seen!
But the Bethlehem star may lead me
To the sight of Him who freed me
From the self that I have been.
Make me pure, Lord: Thou art holy;
Make me meek, Lord: Thou wert lowly;
Now beginning, and alway:
Now begin, on Christmas Day.